M000099591

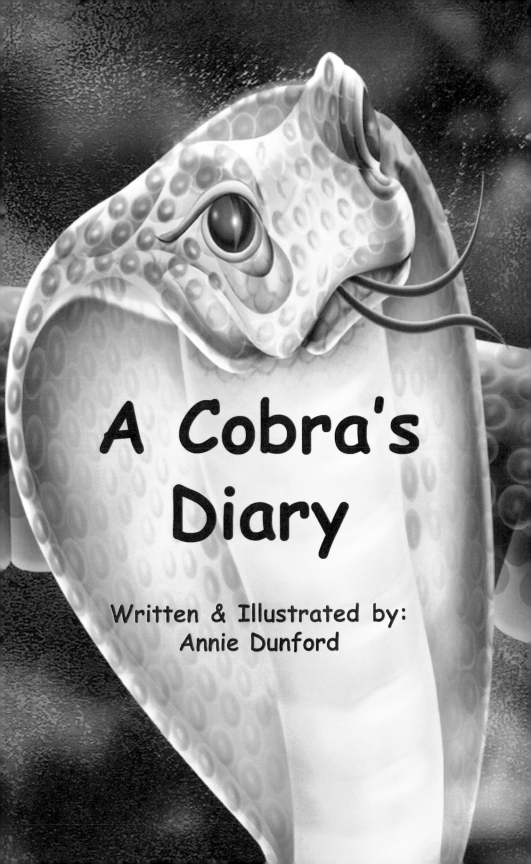

A Cobra's Diary

Written & Illustrated by:
Annie Dunford

Published and printed in the United States of America

First Edition
Dunford, AnnMarie
   A Cobra's Diary/AnnMarie Dunford
   Originally published: Brownsboro, AL.; Just The Box®,
   www.JustTheBox.com
   ISBN: 978-1-4507-4523-9

Layout Design by Mike Dozier, MKADesigns
Printed by Lightning Source, Inc

Dedicated to those who live their dreams.

Good night stars...
Good night moon...
And may you dream of at least six impossible
things before morning...

Hi! My name is Annie and as a ten year old I wrote this story while on the bus, in the car, in the tree house, in my room and wherever I found myself. The story has many characters and reminds me of the many things I see.

Now, I know I write about "revenge", or playing tricks on someone. I would never do anything to hurt them. No one should. We are all different but I do enjoy a good joke or prank and love to laugh. However, anyone who has ever had a brother and sister can relate as you read about Joey, Greg, Sierra, Julianna and I. I hope you enjoy my book.

Annie, Dad and Abby

In a land far, far away...

No really, in a land far, fffaaaarrrr, away...

September 27

Today I am getting ready for Juliana's Birthday party. She is my sister. (Unfortunately). Mom insists on me going with her to Juliana's party at the Scale Salon. Juliana and her friends are getting their scales painted. Uggghhh!!!

She made me floss my fangs and even wax my scales. I don't want to be sitting in a Scale Shop for an hour just watching girls get their scales painted and giggling about weird stuff. I would much rather be with my best friends Joey the lizard and Greg the Blue Jay playing tricks on Sierra the Spider. Our plan for today was to tie her legs up. I guess I can say good-bye to that idea.

October 4

I am so psyched! Joey, Greg, and I all caught up with Sierra and finally got her legs tied up! It was so funny!

We set up a trap and we got Joey to run after her saying "I'm gonna eat you!" She ran into her own web and got stuck. She was squirming for hours. We just sat there and watched. Then of course Juliana came looking

for me, saw what we were doing and ran off in a split second to tell Mom.

We left the scene laughing and went to my house and acted like nothing was going on. Mom stopped us and reared back in her upright position. (Joey and Greg never really like coming to my house. They say that my Mom and Dad scare them and that if they get in trouble they will become dinner.)

Mom asked where Sierra was. We said we didn't know but we saw Sierra outside limping toward our burrow ....and we wondered how did she get out of the web?

Mom brought her in and sent Juliana to get her Mom. Then she sent Joey and Greg home and put me in my room for a good 2 hours.

October 9

Dad and I are going fishing today. Mom made me put on a Snake Vest so that if I fall in it will inflate and I won't die. (She is way too protective).

Dad has always wanted me to go fishing with him but I never really thought I would like it. So we have to bring some kind of tool that takes pictures that mom found from one of the tourists that dropped it, (Greg says it's a camera, but nobody knows.) It is suppose to take pictures, whatever that is, of my first caught fish.

I have never really ever used my fangs and Dad says it's time to start with something easy

like fish. This may not turn out to well. When we got to the stream Dad showed me how to do it correctly.

He says that fish are slippery and really dumb. When I first tried I couldn't decide which fish to catch, they were all so pretty. Dad told me to just pick one for dinner, but I didn't want to harm it.   I just wanted to catch it. Dad then threatened to never let me ever see Greg or Joey again.   So after a few long minutes I did it. Dad was so proud. He took a picture and put the fish in his fangs. We went home and ate it for dinner. I was so glad that it was over.

October 16

Today Joey is going to teach me how to run, but I told him that it probably won't work out that well. He insists that I at least try. So I gave in.

On the first try I fell on top of Joey and knocked him to the ground. He was fine though. Then we both got up and I tried again. This time I fell into the river and nearly drowned. Joey had to jump in and save me.

After that we gave up and now he says that you have to have legs to do anything. It made me upset for a second but I got over it. After that we went to Joey's house for dinner, but I didn't eat because the only appetizing thing there was their pet chipmunk. Otherwise it was all food that had six legs and fried! (DISGUSTING)!

October 23

Today was SCARY from the beginning!

When I woke up Greg was leaning over my bed, staring at me like a zombie. I slowly got up and slithered through the hole to get to the bathroom to brush my fangs, but he followed me.

He chased me down stairs and out to the yard yelling something weird at me. (creepy) He caught up with me and told me that his only pet, Frank the goldfish, had died. He said that he was very depressed and had come to me for help. I didn't exactly know what to do so I took him on a run to take his mind off of it.

We made a very wrong turn and went into the lion's lair. Thank goodness they were asleep, until Greg stepped on a twig and woke the whole group up. We waited for about two seconds and then ran and slithered as fast as our bodies would take us. The hunt was

on! We finally got to the burrow and hid behind Mom. We will NEVER be going near lions again!

October 29

Mom, Juliana and I went shopping for Halloween costumes today. Juliana wants to be a wimpy princess. (ugh girls)

I want to be a GHOST! How scary is that! Mom doesn't want me to be too scary because there are always little animals out and I shouldn't scare them to where they wet themselves! (moms)

I am going to get the most candy award this year at my school. With chocolate covered bugs, banana filled coconuts and even my favorite rat eye chocolate bars!

I am trying to convince mom to let me go trick-or-treating by myself this year, but that is very unlikely.

November 3

Halloween was the best! I won most candy award at my school and mom finally allowed me to go trick-or-treating by myself.

Juliana and her friends got soaked by a hippo running past in the water. HAHAHAHAHAHA! It was hilarious! They ran home screaming and crying because their poor little dresses got muddy and wet.

Meanwhile Joey, Greg and I kept on walking. We were laughing until MARTY came. He was the meanest tiger in school. There were only a few tigers in our school but all were nice except for him. He came over to us and just simply knocked all of our candy out of our bags and that's where I lost it. I reared back and struck. I missed but then Joey and Greg held me back. We were done trick-or-

treating at that point and went home.

November 8

Today I am sick with a stomach ache from eating all of my trick-or-treat candy at Halloween.

Mom made me stay in the burrow all day. I barely got out of bed and did nothing but eat warm rat soup and play my PSP, (Portable Snake Player).

Juliana was home also because she told Mom that if I didn't have to go to school she shouldn't have to either because it wouldn't be fair.

Mom gave in to Juliana and let her stay home. Juliana wasn't much help at all. She turned her boom box up as high as it would go listening to Johnny Rattlebottom - her favorite singer (who I really don't like at all). I finally yelled at her and told her to turn off the music. But of course she ignores me. Today was not a good day.

November 14

Happy Birthday to ME!!!!!! Today is my birthday and I am so excited! Mom, Dad and Juliana said that they have a surprise for me for my birthday!

I hope that they give me the new Snakebox 361! The Snakebox 360 is really old. Now everyone who is anyone has the Snakebox 361! Even Greg and Joey have it.

When I went downstairs Mom had made my favorite breakfast, scrambled toad eggs with bacon and rat tail pancakes. It was the best breakfast ever!

After breakfast our family went to 7 Flags Across Africa the coolest Amusement Park ever! I rode all of the rides! Even the Cheetah! It is the fastest rollercoaster in Africa!

Mom got tired so we had to go home. I was sad that we had to go home but I was just happy that we even went. When we got home I was expecting presents, but Dad said that the trip was my present. I was mad for the rest of the night, but then I realized, I indeed had a great birthday after all.

November 19

Yesterday Dad's boss and co-workers had a goodbye party for their secretary, Mrs. Sarah. She had been working there for 12 years. (Poor lady)

The first and last time I went to dad's office was when mom made me go for "Bring Your Child To Work Day". I never will forget all the screaming and jumping from all the workers and their kids when I was just getting a drink of water. And even Mrs. Heather the hippo passed out because I accidentally slithered over her toe and let me tell you it was not a very pretty sight. Now I know that when a hippo falls over it makes a HUGE mess.

Anyway back to the dinner party. Well first of all I spilled Mango juice on my tuxedo, then I slipped on a banana peel and knocked down one of the waiters and lastly I finished off with flooding the bathroom. Dad was not too happy but I think he forgave me. We went home and went straight to bed.

November 24

Mom took the whole family to the store to get winter scales and tail warmers. I never look forward to going to the store because mom always argues with me about what scale patterns I should get.

On the other hand Juliana always gets what she wants because she is supposedly an angel. So while mom and I are arguing about scales Juliana is in the checkout line. You would think that this whole process would be the other way around but I guess in my family it's just different. Mom and I both finally agreed on plaid and stripes as my winter scale pattern so I guess everyone was happy.

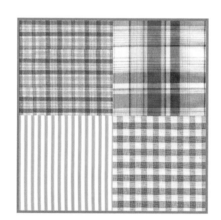

November 29

Yesterday was Thanksgiving and mom made all of our favorite foods like rat-eye soup, fried fish, and a lot more.

By the time I finished eating my stomach was about to burst. Dad loved it almost as much as I did because he was sneaking around the kitchen looking for more dessert.

Juliana didn't eat nearly as much as dad and I did, but she ate some. She even put on her scale pattern that she only wears for really special events.

Mom, Dad and I all wore what we had on that day. We invited a few people to our Thanksgiving dinner like Joey and Greg's families.

We had to invite Mrs. Crouch our neighbor; she is an alligator, so you can imagine how scary it was to eat dinner with her sitting right next to you. She never is really nice but if you don't bother her she will definitely not bother you. We ended up having a great Thanksgiving. I loved it all.

December 6

Winter is here so no one is really ever outside. I can't play with Joey or Greg unless they come over to my house or I go over to theirs.

King Cobra's can still go outside some in the winter because we have to hunt but we usually stay inside. We haven't been doing much since winter started but there is still Christmas coming and the neighborhood Winter Party.

Tomorrow Juliana is having a slumber party with her friends and since I have nothing planned Joey, Greg and I are going to crash it. It is going to be hilarious. Mom and Dad don't know so we have to be super secret about it. Juliana is going to be so mad but this is revenge for when I was sick and she wouldn't turn off her boom box. Wahahahahaha! REVENGE!!!!!!!!!!!

December 12

Our plan succeeded!

We totally crashed Juliana's slumber party! We waited until they were asleep and then we put honey on their faces and sprayed them with whipped cream. (They are the heaviest sleepers known to animal kind.)

After we finished with that we super glued them to their sleeping bags. Once we finished we went to bed. Everything went perfect ...and then Chelsea woke up. (She's one of Juliana's friends) She couldn't get out of

her sleeping bag so she woke Juliana up. (Oh yeah and we videotaped the whole thing by a camera we placed in the corner of the room.)

Everyone then woke up and started screaming and yelling. So then, Mom and Dad had to get involved. And let's just say that it wasn't pretty when they got in there.

We pretended that we were asleep. Mom came in there and got us all up. She dragged us into Juliana's room and asked what happened. We stood there for about 3 seconds with no answer and then we RAN! We sprinted downstairs and to Joey's house. Mom found us about 2 hours later and made us clean up the whole mess. Dad had already got them unglued and cleaned up but we had to clean the room. Let me just say REVENGE IS SWEET!!!!!!

December 19

Today is my last day writing in you because dad thinks that since I am becoming an older snake I should quit writing in a journal. Mom agreed so I guess this is good bye.

Christmas is in 6 days and I am asking for another journal. This doesn't mean that I won't stop writing, it's just I have to stop writing in you. I will never forget you. Juliana and her friends finally got back at Joey, Greg and I.

They gave us a makeover in our sleep. It was horrifying seeing my face covered in eye shadow and lip stick. I spent 3 hours just scrubbing my face and you know what's even worse, mom and dad let them do it so they didn't get in trouble. I hope you never have to suffer through what I've suffered through. So, Good luck!!!